A BEAD
AND A PRAYER

A BEGINNER'S GUIDE
to Protestant Prayer Beads

KRISTEN E. VINCENT

UPPER
ROOM BOOKS®
NASHVILLE

To my parents,
who gave me my first set of prayer beads,
I AM THANKFUL.

To my husband and son,
who have loved me through this journey,
I AM FULFILLED.

To my gracious God,
who created me for this moment in time,
I AM IN AWE.

A BEAD AND A PRAYER

A Beginner's Guide to Protestant Prayer Beads
© 2013 by Kristen E. Vincent. All rights reserved.

The Upper Room website: http://www.upperroom.org
Cover design: Bruce Gore/Gorestudio.com
Cover photos: Kristen E. Vincent

At the time of publication all websites referenced in this book were valid. However, due to the fluid nature of the internet some addresses may have changed, or the content may no longer be relevant.

Scripture quotations not otherwise identified are from the New Revised Standard Version Bible © 1989, Division of Christian Education of the National Council of the Churches of Christ in the United States of America. Used by permission. All rights reserved.

Scripture quotations designated NIV are taken from the Holy Bible, New International Version®, NIV®. Copyright © 1973, 1978, 1984, 2011 by Biblica, Inc.™ Used by permission of Zondervan. All rights reserved worldwide. www.zondervan.com

Scripture quotations designated RSV are from the Revised Standard Version of the Bible, copyright 1952 [2nd edition, 1971] by the Division of Christian Education of the National Council of the Churches of Christ in the United States of America. Used by permission. All rights reserved.

Scripture quotations designated KJV are from the King James Version of the Bible.

LIBRARY OF CONGRESS CATALOGING-IN-PUBLICATION DATA

Vincent, Kristen E.
  A bead and a prayer : a beginner's guide to Protestant prayer beads / Kristen E. Vincent.
      p. cm.
    ISBN 978-0-8358-1217-7 (print)—ISBN 978-0-8358-1218-4 (mobi)—ISBN 978-0-8358-1219-1 (epub)
  1. Beads—Religious aspects. 2. Prayer. I. Title.
  BL619.B43V56 2013
  248.3'2—dc23

                                                              2012041492

Printed in the United States of America

CONTENTS

ACKNOWLEDGMENTS

THIS BOOK IS POSSIBLE because of many people and churches who have joined me in this journey of beads and prayer.

Orange United Methodist Church was my church home when I experienced the call to make prayer beads. Its members were immensely supportive, encouraging, and willing to be the test subjects as I offered up the beads and experimented with ways of talking about them.

Reverend Cyndi McDonald first invited me to lead a workshop on prayer and prayer beads with the women of Marietta First United Methodist Church. Through her leadership and unwavering support I found my voice and the confidence to share this material on a wider basis.

This confidence led me to approach Sherry Elliott in the midst of SOULfeast 2010, The Upper Room's annual spiritual formation retreat. She accepted my offer to teach two workshops on prayer beads for SOULfeast 2011. Both workshops were standing room only, and we realized we were on to something. We have been connected by beads ever since.

This book came into being after discussions with Jeannie Crawford-Lee, Editorial Director for Upper Room Books. Jeannie believed in the idea and offered thoughtful guidance on its development. Her colleague, Rita Collett, project manager, led the editing process with particular skill, humor, and grace, resulting in a beautifully streamlined final product.

Many people were involved in testing the material for this book, including

- Members of two groups from our current church, Allen Memorial United Methodist Church, in Oxford, Georgia: Nancy Bowen, Margie Cline, Pierce Cline (may he rest in peace), Mary B. Flemister, Karen Green, Nancy Henderson, Brandi Gossage, Lyn Gossage, Ellin Knarr, Mary E. Leinweber, Patricia Owens, Carol Penn, Anna Silver, Kayla Vining, Jim Watterson, and Anita Wildman.

- Members of Central United Methodist Church, Concord, North Carolina: Susannah Pittman, Kathy Taylor, Susan Love, Vicki Isenhour, Sherlon Dorton, Margaret Dabbs, Nancy Sanderbeck, Rosey Stein, Karen Johnston, Sue Jones, Jennie Tomlin, and Elaine Braziel.

Acknowledgments

- Participants of the morning session I led during SOUL-Feast 2012: Laura Condra, Koky Elliott, Carol Burrage, Pamela Smith, Carolyn Rochelle, Suzanne LaFever, Leila Niemann, Olive Davenport, Mary Gentry, Linda Stephens, Marion Housel, Ginger Wilkins, Jane Camp, Elaine Jones, Tricia Nowacki, Marietta Smith, Ellen Bibb, Linda Bumgarner, Kathy Houser, Vernagaye Sullivan, Philip L. Holcombe, and Barbara Page Kell.
- A number of the Prayerworks Studio Facebook fans, as well as the women of The Circle of Friends Evening Group of Hallied United Methodist Church, Chippewa Falls, Wisconsin, who tested the bead-making instructions and provided suggestions to ensure they were user-friendly.

In addition, Rabbi Dan Gordon shared his remarkable gift of storytelling to help me understand the use of the Jewish prayer shawl and its knotted fringe.

CeCe Nickolich, my spiritual director, offered abiding love and wise, Spirit-filled guidance that helped me to trust the God who has faithfully called me to this journey.

The leadership team and participants of the Academy for Spiritual Formation have all helped me to be still. That stillness has led to profound moments of healing, encounters with God, and insights into this calling.

Without knowing it, my parents, Brent and Barbara Johnson, set this journey in motion with their gift of prayer beads many years ago. Through them I have experienced a deep love that comes from shared joys and hardships, a love of God, and a fondness for good Mexican food. They have dubbed themselves my Texas marketing division and are two of my biggest encouragers. I love them immensely.

Most of all, there was my husband, Max, and son, Matthew. About ten days after I experienced my call to make prayer beads I gathered the courage to share it with Max. Rather than laugh or ask for a divorce, he simply said, "Makes sense." Since then, he and Matthew have gotten used to finding random beads on the floor, making do while I'm away at retreats or meeting writing deadlines, and enduring my routine requests to review drafts. Through everything they have offered their unconditional love, theological insight, and inspired humor. I am the better for it. Hopefully, this book is too.

INTRODUCTION

"I think our lives are saying that we need
some sacred spaces and sacred things in them.
We need some things that are as mysterious
as the Mystery itself."

—ROBERT BENSON
Living Prayer

IN 1990 MY PARENTS went on a mission trip to the
Dominican Republic, returning with a number of gifts
for me. I loved each of them. But about three or four
months later, my mom came to me with a little box in
her hand. She explained that she had purchased one other
gift for me on the trip, though she felt unsure I would
like it and so had delayed giving it to me. Tentatively, she
offered the box. Inside was a circle of ten wooden, hand-
carved beads with a cross. I recognized that this was a
kind of mini-rosary.

I found the gift surprising on two fronts. First, my family was not Catholic. At the time we were Presbyterian

and, like all good Calvinists, we had no stained-glass windows in our church, no icons on our walls, and certainly no rosaries in our hands. As a result, my mother's choosing to give me a rosary did take me aback, though only to a degree. By high school I had developed a passion for the church, and I had recently graduated from college with a major in religion. My mother's gift acknowledged what was important to me.

The second surprise came in my reaction to the beads. They captivated me. I sat for the longest time, fingering the beads, studying their shapes, marveling at the craftsmanship and the beauty of the design. As I did, I felt a great sense of *awe* deep within me to this small set of beads. No other word could describe my response. What touched me most was the thought that people used these beads to pray to God. As I held the beads, I realized that people all around the world were using similar beads to connect with the Divine. I felt a strong link to God and to them—a moment of surprising communion. Suffice it to say, I was smitten with this gift.

I don't remember whether I talked much about that first rosary or not, but somehow my mom got the message that with this little rosary she had hit pay dirt in terms of gift ideas for me. From that time on she brought back rosaries from her travels. Soon, other friends and family did the same. Over time I have gathered rosaries from all over the world: Mexico, Honduras, Guatemala, Costa Rica, Italy, Spain, Israel, France, England, Hungary, Ireland, and the United States. I have a rosary blessed by the pope as well as a rosary blessed in Bethlehem's Church of the Nativity. As my rosary collection grew I began to develop an interest in other items that people use to pray to God: icons, *retablos* (Latin American devotional paintings), prayer ropes, *milagros* (religious folk charms), and holding crosses. I added those to my collection as well.

While I enjoyed displaying these items and talking with others about them, I didn't use them to pray. Truthfully, I wasn't praying much at all. Even though I went on to receive a master of theological studies degree, marry a United Methodist minister, and remain involved in the church, I didn't have a prayer life to speak of. I struggled with prayer. I felt awkward. I never knew what words to say and thought surely God had better things to do than listen to me prattle on about whatever. I wonder now if I had amassed this collection of prayer tools in the hopes of living vicariously through these objects and the prayers of those who used them.

That all changed in July 2009 when I experienced a slightly quirky calling to make rosaries. For the next few days I pondered the experience. I even Googled "how to make a rosary." But mostly I wondered if God had *really* called me down this path. It seemed pretty peculiar. But I couldn't explain away the fact that this experience of call had named my passion for prayer tools and invited me to act on this. This call came despite the fact that I hadn't paid much attention to prayer tools in a while. I was kept busy raising a son, planning Sunday school studies, and working as a nonprofit consultant. So I kept the experience to myself and continued to ponder and research.

A few days later I came across a website that talked about Anglican prayer beads: in effect, prayer beads for Protestants. I had never heard of them. That's when I understood the purpose of my calling. I was not being called to make Catholic rosaries. I was being called to make and share these "Protestant" prayer beads.

Since then I have made, sold, or given away more than four thousand sets of prayer beads. I started a blog and began writing devotions for prayer beads and relating their history. That led to public-speaking opportunities and leading retreats and workshops on prayer beads—which led to the writing of this book.

Response from the public has been fantastic and humbling. People can't get enough of the prayer beads. They purchase a set for themselves, then come back to buy multiple sets as gifts for others. They come to me with stories—

wonderful testimonies—of how the prayer beads have enhanced their relationship with God. The prayer beads have taken on a life of their own. Clearly people hunger for new (and ancient) ways of connecting with God.

Meanwhile, I began using the beads in prayer. I started tentatively, holding the beads one at a time and offering up particular prayer requests and events for which I was thankful. Gaining confidence, I experimented with ways of using the beads to praise, to confess, to intercede, and to offer thanks. Eventually, I practiced listening with the beads. Over time, I realized I had become comfortable with prayer. Odds are this was the real purpose of my calling—and the real gift of the prayer beads.

———————————

I designed this Bible study to introduce prayer beads to Christians who have no experience in using them. I focus on Protestants since we have not been taught or encouraged to use prayer beads. This study exists for the curious ones who want to know how to use beads in prayer and for the anxious ones who worry about whether it is okay to use them. It is for the experienced ones who want to learn more about their history and use and for everyone in between.

Prayer beads are a tool for prayer. Just as a hammer and nails help us construct a house, so prayer beads help us construct a life of connection with God. The beads are not the end; they are the means to an end, which is communion with God. I want to emphasize that prayer beads are just one of many tools to assist in prayer. Not everyone needs a prayer tool. Many people feel comfortable with prayer and have developed ways of praying that work well for them. If you are among them, I invite you to continue reading to learn more about the history and use of this ancient Christian prayer practice. However, many people struggle with prayer. Their minds wander; they get bored; they wonder if they are being heard; they struggle with what to say. Prayer beads can help them develop rich lives of prayer, deepening their connection with God. This book will offer ways of doing that.

Throughout the next four weeks we will explore the history and art of using beads in prayer. The first two weeks will focus on answering two major questions: *Why* should we consider using prayer beads? Is it really okay for Protestants to use beads in prayer? Once we have addressed these questions we will spend weeks three and four considering *how* to use prayer beads. We will start by exploring various ways to use beads in prayer. In particular, we will look at ways to use the beads to help deepen our faith and our understanding of what we as Christians believe. Then we will consider how prayer beads can help us listen for what God has to say to us.

Each week's lesson has four components. We will begin with a Scripture Passage, which leads to the Weekly Reading. The reading will take no more than twenty to thirty minutes per week. After the reading, I provide a Prayer Bead Experience. These exercises introduce various approaches to praying with beads and the discovery of meaningful uses. If possible, practice the experiences at least once every day.

At the close of each week, I offer Reflection Questions for personal and group use. The questions will increase our understanding of the week's study and the Prayer Bead Experience.

Each of the four weeks has a theme that illustrates and underscores the purpose and benefits of prayer beads. The themes are as follows: encounter, surrender, offer, and listen. Prayer beads can help us *encounter* God in all of God's glory. When we do, we *surrender* to God's power and call to communion. Our response to the surrendering encourages us to *offer* ourselves to God, including the concerns that are on our heart. At that point, we stop to *listen* for God's response. In that moment, we hear God's word to us.

In our busy, noisy lives we can easily miss one or more of these elements. When we do, we begin to feel lost and hopeless. We wonder where God is and whether God hears our prayers. Prayer beads can help us enter into and maintain lives of prayer that are whole and complete.

I invite you to take up your beads and join me on our journey together in prayer. When you do, I pray you will be filled with God's perfect and gracious love.

Before You Get Started

A Note about the Beads

Prayer beads of many types exist throughout the world. For this study's purposes I will focus primarily on the Protestant prayer beads I mentioned earlier.

Protestant prayer beads are made up of a cross or other pendant and thirty-three or more beads. One large bead, called the "invitatory" bead, reminds us that God invites us to a time of prayer. We can use this bead to begin our prayer, much like churches employ a call to worship to begin a church service.

In addition to the large invitatory bead, we find four more large beads. When we splay out a set of Protestant prayer beads, these beads form the four points of a cross and thus are called "cruciform" beads. Beyond representing the points of the cross, the number 4 reminds us of the four Gospels, the four seasons of the year, the four parts of our day (morning, afternoon, evening, and night), and the four directions (north, south, east, and west).

Between each of the cruciform beads is a set of seven smaller beads. Because a week has seven days, these beads are called "week" beads. Like the number 4, the number 7 has bountiful meaning for Christians:

The church calendar consists of seven seasons (Advent, Christmas, Epiphany, Lent, Easter, Pentecost, and Ordinary Time);

Genesis tells us there were seven days of Creation; on the seventh day God rested, calling us also to keep it holy;

In John's Gospel, Jesus makes seven "I AM" statements:

1. "I AM the bread of life" (6:35, 48).
2. "I AM the light of the world" (8:12; 9:5).
3. "I AM the gate for the sheep" (10:7).
4. "I AM the good shepherd" (10:11, 14).
5. "I AM the resurrection and the life" (11:25).
6. "I AM the way, and the truth, and the life" (14:6).
7. "I AM the true vine" (15:1, 5).

The number 7 shows up often in the book of Revelation, including John's note that his letter is addressed to the "seven churches" (1:4); and both Jews and Christians believe the number 7 symbolizes spiritual perfection.

When we add together the one invitatory bead, the four cruciform beads, and the twenty-eight week beads we get a total of thirty-three beads. The group that developed this format (page 47) appreciated this number since it represented Jesus' life on earth for thirty-three years.

For the first year, I chose to use that number of beads. However, over time I began to desire some representation of the fact that Christ still lives today, particularly since the Resurrection is the hallmark of the Christian faith. So, I added one more bead, positioning it between the invitatory bead and the bottom cruciform bead. I call it the "resurrection" bead and use it in my prayers to focus on Christ's gift to us of eternal life. Adding this bead makes the total number of beads thirty-four. However, I still tell people that Protestant prayer beads are comprised of thirty-three beads, which represent Jesus' life and ministry on earth—plus one bead to represent his resurrection.

The format looks like this:

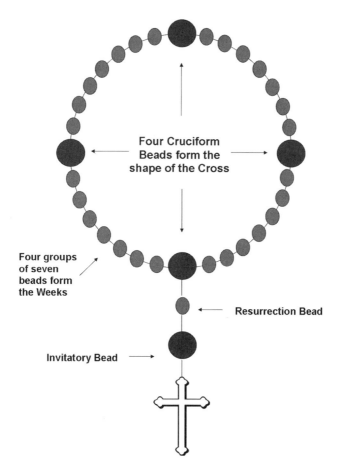

Four Cruciform
Beads form the
shape of the Cross

Four groups
of seven
beads form
the Weeks

Resurrection Bead

Invitatory Bead

I want to emphasize that there is no right or wrong way to make your prayer beads. This study will focus on the Protestant prayer bead format of thirty-four beads; however, you may design your own format as I did and modify the Prayer Bead Experiences accordingly. Since this is your prayer tool, it should be meaningful for you and for your time with the Lord.

This study assumes that you have a set of prayer beads. You can complete the study without a set, but you will miss out on the Prayer Bead Experiences and the intent of this study, which is to lead you through an exploration of the use of the beads in prayer. You can purchase a set of Protestant prayer beads. Resources (page 105) lists many websites where you can do this.

However, I strongly encourage you to begin by making your *own* set for two reasons. First, the process of making your own set of prayer beads can be an avenue to connect with God. The very act of choosing your beads—the size, the color, the texture—inspires you to think about this tool you will use to encounter the Divine. You might choose colors that have meaning or carry memories for you. You could incorporate beads from a family heirloom or a souvenir from a special trip. Once you have chosen your beads, you will begin to string them together on the wire or thread. As you do, reflect on the ways God connects us together for a higher purpose, just as the beads are strung together to form a complete set of prayer beads. Once you have finished, these beads will have additional meaning for you given that you have made them for the purpose of communing with God.

The second reason is that the process affords an uplifting group activity and serves to introduce the study. The field testers enjoyed the camaraderie, the interaction, the collective creative process, and the shared excitement about this new way of praying. So, while I can't mandate that you make your own prayer beads, whether individually or as a group, I can strongly encourage you to make this a part of your study. Add an extra week to this study and use the first meeting to let the group members make their own beads.

I have included instructions (page 89) in the back of the book, along with suggestions for where to purchase materials. My company, Prayerworks Studio, also offers prayer bead kits, which include all the necessary materials to make a set of prayer beads. I have also uploaded a video tutorial to guide you in making your own set at http://abeadnaprayer.wordpress.com/2013/05/02/video-how-to-make-prayer-beads/.

WEEK ONE

Why Prayer Beads?

ENCOUNTER

If we do not pray,
we fail to realize
that we are in
the presence of God.
—KARL BARTH
Prayer

Scripture Passage

The LORD said to Moses: Speak to the Israelites, and tell them to make fringes on the corners of their garments throughout their generations and to put a blue cord on the fringe at each corner. You have the fringe so that, when you see it, you will remember all the commandments of the LORD and do them, and not follow the lust of your own heart and your own eyes. So you shall remember and do all my commandments, and you shall be holy to your God. I am the LORD your God, who brought you out of the land of Egypt, to be your God: I am the LORD your God (Num. 15:37-41).

Weekly Reading

One obvious question about prayer beads is Why? Why prayer beads? Why in the world do we need something to help us pray? Prayer is such a simple thing. Whether we kneel or sit or stand or dance; whether we pray silently or out loud. Whether we read scripture, say prayers written by someone else, or offer our own words, we should not need something to aid our time with God. Right?

If only it were that easy. Clearly, it is not; otherwise everyone would "pray without ceasing."

A lot of people struggle with prayer. As I mentioned earlier, I never knew what to say to God. If I heard of someone's illness, grief, or job loss, I would pray, "Lord, please help (*fill in the blank*)." Otherwise, I felt unsure about what God wanted to hear. I did not want to fill up the space with empty words, but I also did not want to spend too much time talking about myself. Were my words worthy of God's time and attention? In the end, I just skipped praying altogether.

I know I am not alone in my struggle with prayer. I know it because I go to church. That is where you will find a lot of people who do not know how to pray. Sure, we can recite the Lord's Prayer and the prayers in the hymnal with ease. We can handle communal prayers, particularly those that are familiar or written down for us. But call on one of us to pray out loud, individually, and—heaven forbid—extemporaneously, and you will hear crickets. Or suggest to a friend who has just shared a specific prayer concern that the two of you pray together, and you may be left to wonder how your friend made such a hasty exit. We are uncomfortable with prayer.

Luckily for us, God knows our limitations. God calls us into relationship. God knows we accept the call in the midst of our insecurities, our frazzled lives, our egocentricities, and our sin. God knows we bring all that with us to the table. The Lord acknowledges our inability to focus and our inadequacies. So God provides tools to aid us in prayer. Look at what God does for the Israelites.

Here the Israelites are really struggling. God has delivered them from slavery and led them out of Egypt, promising to bring them to the land of milk and honey. But the trip is taking too long. The Israelites have been in the desert for years and are beginning to lose hope. Will they ever see the Promised Land? Will they ever settle down and experience stability again? Will they ever have anything to eat besides manna? Their days have been filled with wandering. So much wandering. And hunger, death, and attempted invasions. A person—and a people—can only take so much. Recognizing this limitation, God commands Moses to "put [God's] name on" (Num. 6:27) the Israelites and share the following blessing:

The Lord bless you and keep you;
the Lord make his face to shine upon you,
    and be gracious to you;
the Lord lift up his countenance upon you,
    and give you peace" (Num. 6:24-26).

On this momentous occasion, God blesses the Israelites and places God's name on them, signifying divine care and provision for this journey to the Promised Land.

And for a while the people accept this word. They settle down and enjoy the favor of God's blessings. But that enjoyment doesn't last.

Apparently, the Israelites forget God's blessing and again start feeling hopeless. They begin to rebel. Like children who do not get their way, the Israelites initiate a collective temper tantrum by whining and complaining. They even question and mock the Lord, stating that they would have been better off in captivity. In case their displeasure isn't evident through their words, they begin to break the commandments, the very laws God has given for their protection and for defining them as a nation, a chosen people. In the passage immediately preceding today's scripture passage, one Israelite has even dared to work on the sabbath. Things are getting out of hand.

God tries several times to meet the Israelites in the midst of their confusion, employing various methods to address their behavior. God berates and disciplines, encourages and reasons. But by Numbers 15:37, God employs a different tactic. Moses is to instruct the Israelites to "make fringes on the corners of their garments." Really? Fringe? What difference will that make?

Granted, fringe on a garment would not have seemed odd in ancient times. In both Egypt and Assyria garments with fringe were customary. Indeed, in some cultures, wearing fringe signaled nobility. It even carried great meaning: People believed that if you held on to someone's fringe when making a request, the person could not deny the request. You may recall the New Testament story of the hemorrhaging woman who touched Jesus' garment so that she would be healed. Sure enough, Jesus turned and declared her healed. (See Matthew 9:20-22 and Mark 5:25-34.) We may assume the woman had grabbed the fringe on Jesus' robe.

The Israelites heed God's instructions and add fringe to their garments. Following further instructions in Deuteronomy 22:12, they tie the fringe into knots, called *tzitzit*. These are not average knots; each set of fringe contains five knots made from eight strands of thread. There is an art—filled with meaning and ritual—to tying them. Like the Protestant prayer beads, great symbolism is attached to the numbers associated with the knots. The number paired with the Hebrew word for *tzitzit* is 600. When you add that to the five knots and eight strands you get 613, which equals the total number of commandments in the Old Testament. By wearing and fingering the knots, the Jews stay closely connected to the God who calls them to obedience through these commandments.

Over time, the Jews tried to assimilate into the prevailing culture because of persecution and/or a desire to fit in, causing many to stop wearing the knotted fringe on their outer garments. Instead, they opted to wear prayer shawls, called *tallith*, which included the fringe. Centuries later, they developed a type of shirt with fringe to be worn under their clothes. Many Jews still wear this today.

So, the wearing of fringe is not the odd part of this story. The oddity comes in God's taking this seemingly insignificant accessory and infusing it with great meaning. In fact, as we learn from our reading, God intends the fringe to have multiple purposes. First, as a visual cue; God says that when the Israelites see the fringe, they will remember. Remember what? The commandments that God has given them—all of them.

There's more. It is not enough to *remember* the commandments. The Israelites need to *do* them too. Remembering the commandments and doing them will keep the Israelites from following their own desires. Remembering the commandments and doing them will silence the "lust" of their hearts, and they can stay out of trouble.

It gets better. If the Israelites successfully use this tool in a disciplined manner, they will become holy. God has given them the commandments for a reason; obeying them becomes a form of worship that leads to holiness—and the fringe helps them get there!

From the Israelites' perspective, as they stand in the midst of their pain and rebellion in that barren desert, it may seem that God is messing with them by offering them fringe—some divine joke. It probably takes a while before they can recognize the fringe as divine gift.

The fringe provided a tangible means of reaching across the chasm and reconnecting with a God they loved but could not see or understand. They could hold the fringe and be reminded of God's blessing upon them. God met the Israelites in the midst of their tantrums, railings, anxiety, and bad behavior and offered them a way out. Using this prayer tool would remind the Israelites of who God is and who they were in relation to God—a people chosen and blessed by God. No matter what happened, they were going to be okay.

Prayer beads work in the same fashion. They can help us find our way to God. How? Like the fringe of the Jews, prayer beads serve as a visual cue on many levels. On one hand, they can remind us to pray. I have heard many people attest to this fact. In the middle of a busy day or at bedtime, they will look down, see their prayer beads, and be reminded to pray. They will bring to mind God's presence, which calls them into an encounter. Such a visual cue has distinct importance for someone in the midst of crisis or doubt. In that moment of darkness, the beads can serve as a powerful reminder that God is present, encouraging that person to "fear not."

Along with the visual cue, we cannot deny the tangible effect of the beads. We can touch them, hold on to them. We can close our eyes and feel the shape and texture of the beads. We can follow the path of the beads as they guide us up and away from the cross, around the circle, and finally to rest back at the cross. This benefit should not be quickly dismissed. It offers a valuable way to focus our minds if our thoughts are scattered or we are praying in a noisy environment. Should our minds start to wander during prayer—to the grocery list or the disagreement we had with our children—the feel of the beads can bring us back to the moment at hand: connection with God. In those moments of darkness, when we wonder about God's presence, the beads serve as a concrete sign of God with us.

For those who struggle with how to pray—or what to pray—prayer beads can provide much-needed structure. Protestant prayer beads, made up of four sets of seven beads, can make prayer easier, especially for hesitant prayers. Rather than having to think of a whole prayer, they can break it down into four bite-sized pieces. For example, they can employ the first set of seven beads to praise God, using each of the seven beads to think of something to say in praise of who God is. The second set can be for confession. The third set can be for our intercessions—

our joys and concerns—and the fourth for thanksgiving for what God has done in our lives. There you have it: instant prayer. I call this "The Full Circle Prayer."[1] It provides a priceless introduction to prayer as well as to prayer beads. Many other approaches use the structure of the beads to form our prayers. I have listed some examples in "More Devotions for Prayer Beads" (page 99). Feel free to create your own.

Children take to beads like ducks to water. They like the pretty colors and textures, the feel of the beads in their hands. And the structure does wonders for them as they craft their prayers. I often use "chaplets," minisets of prayer beads made up of two sets of seven beads, when I work with children. They can use one set to "bless" the people in their lives, while the second set can be used to talk to God. Or they can use the first seven beads to tell God what they are thankful for and the second set what they hope for.

A friend of mine gave a chaplet to her three-year-old daughter. She reported that the child ran around the house holding her prayer beads and saying, "I can talk to Jesus." Prayer beads make prayer accessible to children who are doing their best to worship a God they cannot see or fathom. (See page 103 for a sample prayer bead devotion for children.)

As we begin to practice with beads in prayer we will experience these benefits and possibly others as well. The beauty of prayer beads surfaces in the many ways we can employ this insignificant set of beads to connect with the Divine. And when we do, we will encounter God and be reminded that God is with us. Like the Israelites, we will know that we are going to be okay.

Prayer Bead Experience

This week's experience will help you encounter God as you become more familiar with your prayer beads.

Pray "The Full Circle Prayer." As you do, focus on the four sets of seven beads in the Protestant prayer bead format. Practice following the path of the beads as they lead you toward God. Let the varying sizes or textures of the beads guide you in prayer. Practice this Prayer Bead Experience daily, then come together with a group at the end of the week to share your thoughts and reactions.

The Full Circle Prayer

Cross: Loving God,

Invitatory bead: you have called me into this time of prayer,

Resurrection bead: to be with you.

First cruciform bead: I praise you, Lord, for. . . .

Week beads, set 1: Use each bead to praise God; think of different qualities of God for which you would want to give praise.

Second cruciform bead: I ask, Lord, for your forgiveness for. . . .

Week beads, set 2: Use each bead to confess your sins to God.

Third cruciform bead: I pray, Lord, for. . . .

Week beads, set 3: Use each bead to list your intercessions—your joys and concerns for yourself or others.

Fourth cruciform bead: I thank you, Lord, for. . . .

Week beads, set 4: Use each bead to offer thanks to God for the blessings in your life.

Resurrection bead: Christ is alive in me.

Invitatory bead: Thanks be to God.

Cross: Amen.

REFLECTION QUESTIONS

• When has an unlikely item brought to your mind a sense of God's presence? How have you used that item to remind you of that experience at other times?

- How would an ordinary item, like fringe, move you to think of God?
- What benefits do you see in the use of prayer beads?
- How could prayer beads help someone who is new to or uncomfortable with prayer?
- How could prayer beads assist someone who is already comfortable with prayer?
- How can prayer beads help you encounter God?
- What thoughts and reactions did you have to the Prayer Bead Experience?

Week Two

Why Prayer Beads for Protestants?

SURRENDER

They are the things, the earthly things,
that remind you to pay attention for the Voice
and to trust that it will speak to you.
They are the things of this world
that remind you of the world beyond.

—Robert Benson

Living Prayer

Scripture Passage

But we appeal to you, brothers and sisters, to respect those who labor among you, and have charge of you in the Lord and admonish you; esteem them very highly in love because of their work. Be at peace among yourselves. And we urge you, beloved, to admonish the idlers, encourage the fainthearted, help the weak, be patient with all of them. See that none of you repays evil for evil, but always seek to do good to one another and to all. Rejoice always, pray without ceasing, give thanks in all circumstances; for this is the will of God in Christ Jesus for you. Do not quench the Spirit. Do not despise the words of prophets, but test everything; hold fast to what is good; abstain from every form of evil (1 Thess. 5:12-22).

Weekly Reading

Many Protestants think that using beads to pray is strictly a Catholic ritual. We have seen our Catholic friends with their rosaries and may even have admired them from afar. Otherwise, we have kept our distance. We do not know why we Protestants do not use beads, but surely there is a good reason for it. It turns out, however, that the use of beads in prayer is part of our heritage too.

We often forget that Protestants and Catholics share the same lineage and history in which the practice of using beads or something similar in prayer goes way back—all the way back to the early church.

The church in Thessalonica is developing nicely. Paul had spent only three weeks in the city, preaching and introducing the Thessalonians to the risen Christ before the Jews ran him out of town. Three weeks was hardly enough time to establish the work of the church. Yet, despite all odds, it is growing and thriving. Paul has so anxiously awaited news about the new church that he sends Timothy to check on it. Timothy returns with glowing reports of strong faith and love for Christ.

Still, all is not perfect. Timothy also reports that the new Christians have taken Paul's message about the second coming of Christ a little too seriously. They have quit their jobs and slacked off on their responsibilities, expecting Christ's return at any minute. Divisions are occurring within the church. Many of them don't trust their religious leaders. The threat remains that this young church will be corrupted by the prevailing pagan customs.

Like any new converts (and even we old converts), the Thessalonians need nurture and encouragement. That's what Paul wants to give them. Paul emphasizes the qualities that will strengthen their lives as Christians. He offers a laundry list of words, including *respect*, *esteem*, *peace*, *admonish*, *encourage*, *help*, *patient*, and *good*.

At the crux of the message, Paul makes three appeals: rejoice always, pray without ceasing, give thanks in all circumstances. Notice the verbs Paul uses: *rejoice*, *pray*, *give thanks*. They are positive and simple. Paul calls on Christians to be joyful, to pray, and to be thankful. Joyful, praying, and thankful people do not disrespect their leaders. They don't bicker or slack off. They certainly don't repay evil for evil. But it is not enough to be joyful, to pray, and to be thankful *sometimes*. If we implement these characteristics only some of the time, we are choosing less beneficial behaviors the rest of the time. Paul insists that we do these things always, without ceasing, in all circumstances. Only then will we maintain our constant connection with God. It is from this place of connection with God that the Thessalonians' actions must flow.

Paul's emphasis on prayer forms the heart of this passage. Through prayer, the Thessalonians will surrender to God. Their remembrance of who God is and what God has done for them will strengthen their faith and undergird every thought and action. It will prevent bad behavior, address doubt, and handle fear. And it will, necessarily, lead to rejoicing and thanksgiving, especially if it is done without ceasing.

Paul recognizes the difficulty of being a Christian. The Thessalonian Christians who are new in the faith and still trying to understand what it means to follow Christ face an extremely arduous task. They need all the help they can get to grow in their faith. Paul admonishes them to pray without ceasing so they will thrive.

Prayer was central to the early church as well as integral to its growth. In Acts 2:46 we learn that the earliest Christians spent "much time together in the temple," praying and worshiping God. And Acts 6:4 tells us that the disciples devoted themselves to prayer. But in the third century CE, a number of Christians decided to take it up a notch. They left the hustle and bustle of the cities and towns and moved to the desert. They sought a quieter place to live, one where they could devote their lives entirely to unceasing prayer. These desert dwellers—our first monks and nuns—became known as the desert fathers and mothers.

In their effort to pray unceasingly, many of these early monastics began praying all 150 Psalms on a daily basis.[2] This consistency of prayer enabled these dedicated men and women to memorize the Psalms, an impressive feat by any measure. However, reciting the entire Psalter by memory requires a way to keep track of where you are. To address this concern, the monks and nuns kept 150 small pebbles or stones in their pocket or in a bowl. This helped them keep track of where they were in their recitation. But pebbles, though small, aren't the easiest or lightest-weight tool to cart around, particularly if you pray as you walk or work or move about. So, not surprisingly, by the fourth century the desert fathers and mothers had begun to use a prayer rope made of knots that must have been much lighter and easier to carry.

Use of the prayer rope continued until sometime around the Middle Ages. By then, priests, monks, and nuns had developed a new way of praying without ceasing. They observed a schedule of prayers throughout the day and night known as the Divine, or Daily Office. The Office involved services of prayer seven times throughout the day and night and required the use of multiple books, including the Bible and a hymnal. Many of the laity who lived around the monasteries and churches witnessed this discipline and wanted to participate. However, illiteracy was widespread. The laypeople could not read the books or follow the order of service.

To provide a way for laypeople to share in this prayer discipline, church leadership encouraged them to recite the Lord's Prayer 150 times. This would equal the number of Psalms and provide another way of praying without ceasing—a great idea in terms of simplicity. Everyone knew the Lord's Prayer and could certainly recite it multiple times. The challenge came in keeping up with whether you were on Lord's Prayer #27 or Lord's Prayer #131. People needed a tracking tool for the repetitions. Someone introduced a string of beads for use during this prayer time. The strand, made up of 150 beads, was divided into sets of ten beads. These beads—as well as this form of prayer—became known as "the rosary," though it was also commonly known as "the poor man's Psalter."

This is the common heritage between Protestants and Catholics: our ancestors and our history as Christians. So why don't Protestants use the rosary today? In 1517 Martin Luther aired his grievances with the church and unwittingly sparked a firestorm of events now known as the Protestant Reformation. Hard as I've tried, I haven't managed to find many historical accounts of how Luther and his fellow reformers regarded the rosary. I found one reference in Luther's 1535 article "A Simple Way to Pray," written for his barber, Peter Beskendorf. In sharing his ideas for prayer, Luther admonishes Peter to avoid simply reciting words, which is like "idle chatter and prattle, read word for word out of a book, as were the rosaries by the laity."[3] Some people have cited this reference to argue that Luther was anti-rosary; however, I think that misses his point. I believe Luther's concern centered less on the rosary than on prayer that is devoid of feeling and faith. Luther is warning against *empty prayer*, rather than the use of the rosary itself.

Nan Lewis Doerr and Virginia Stem Owens support this view in their book *Praying with Beads: Daily Prayers for the Christian Year*. They mention that after Luther's split from the Catholic Church, he did not forbid Protestants' use of the rosary. By then, use of the rosary included repetitions of both the Lord's Prayer and the Hail Mary prayer. Luther modified the Hail Mary prayer,[4] leaving only those words that are found in scripture. His taking the time to pursue this endeavor implies his valuing of the rosary as a prayer tool.

Some of his fellow reformers, including John Calvin, disagreed. They wanted people to relate directly with God, allowing nothing to stand in the way, including religious statues, stained-glass windows, icons, and prayer beads.[5] They probably knew that old habits were hard to break. It would have been difficult for people to use the rosary without saying the traditional Hail Mary prayer. So the use of beads in prayer ended up on the cutting-room floor, along with the icons and stained glass. Since then, we Protestants have been raised to think that prayer beads are strictly for Catholics.

But in the 1980s, a pioneering group of Episcopalians in Texas decided to right that wrong. During a study of contemplative prayer, the group focused on ancient prayer practices, including ways of praying without ceasing. By the end of their study, they had developed a new form of prayer beads that they called "Anglican prayer beads" or the "Anglican rosary." This new rosary would differ from its Catholic counterpart in that no set way of praying with the beads was prescribed. And rather than being made up of sets of ten beads, the Anglican prayer bead set had four sets of seven beads. Like its counterpart, the Anglican rosary would provide a visual cue and structure to prayer. And in so doing, it would make it easier to pray without ceasing. Protestants once again had a way of praying with beads.

This brief history lesson helps us understand that prayer beads are not taboo for Protestants or anyone else. They are one tool of many for use in prayer. God calls us to constant relationship through unceasing prayer. Prayer beads are a way of doing that.

One remarkable fact I have learned on this journey surrounds the etymology of our English word *bead*. It derives from the Old English word *bede*, which means "prayer." Over the course of time, beads have been used so widely and so effectively in prayer that the very word *bead* has come to mean "prayer." Edmund Spenser wrote in his sixteenth-century book *The Faerie Queen*,

> All night she spent in bidding of her bedes,
> And all the day in doing good and godly deedes.

Let us take up our "bedes" unceasingly, to surrender to the God who created us. And in so doing, let us fill our days with good and godly deeds.

Prayer Bead Experience

This week's experience centers on discipline and is designed to help you pray "unceasingly" in the manner of the early Christians, so that you can surrender to God's call.

I offer two choices. Try one or both. Experience the use of beads in prayer repetition. Observe how you feel as you repeat the prayers over and over. Consider how and whether this discipline of repeating the same prayer enhances or otherwise affects your time with God.

For this approach to function, pay no attention to the different types of beads in the Protestant prayer bead format. Instead, recite the same prayer for each bead in your strand. Practice this Prayer Bead Experience every day, then come together as a group at the end of the week to share your thoughts and reactions.

The Jesus Prayer

The prayer ropes developed by the desert fathers and mothers are still in use to this day in the Eastern Church. In the Greek Orthodox Church they are called *komboskini* (which in Greek means "a rope with knots") and in the Russian Orthodox Church people refer to them as *chotki*. Typically, prayer ropes consist of thirty-three, fifty, or one hundred knots made out of black wool. The color black reminds us of the mystery of God and our faith, while the wool reminds us that we are members of Jesus' flock. The number 33 represents the years Jesus spent on earth. The number 100 symbolizes the fullness of Creation.

People today use prayer ropes to recite the Jesus Prayer. This short, simple prayer is over fifteen centuries old and serves as a glorious profession of faith. It is recited once for each knot in the prayer rope. Using your prayer beads, repeat the prayer with each bead.

> Lord Jesus Christ, Son of God,
> have mercy on me, a sinner.

The Lord's Prayer

The rosary was developed to enable illiterate Christians to participate in a specific spiritual discipline. They used each bead to recite the Lord's Prayer. You may be familiar with this prayer and may even say it on a regular basis.

However, experience what it is like to repeat this prayer, over and over again, using your beads. Repeat the prayer once with each bead.

Our Father, who art in heaven,
hallowed be thy name.
Thy kingdom come,
thy will be done on earth as it is in heaven.
Give us this day our daily bread.
And forgive us our trespasses,
as we forgive those who trespass against us.
And lead us not into temptation,
but deliver us from evil.
For thine is the kingdom, and the power,
and the glory, forever. Amen.

Reflection Questions

- Prior to reading this book, what were your thoughts about the Catholic rosary?
- Do you think it is okay for Protestants to use beads in prayer? Why or why not?
- How can prayer be a discipline?
- What does it mean to you to "pray without ceasing"?

- How could using beads aid your ability to pray without ceasing?
- What thoughts and reactions did you have to the Prayer Bead Experience?

WEEK THREE

How to Use Prayer Beads

OFFER

To believe that God can reach us and bless us
in the ordinary junctures of daily life
is the stuff of prayer.
—RICHARD J. FOSTER
Prayer: Finding the Heart's True Home

A Bead and a Prayer

Scripture Passage

Are any among you suffering? They should pray. Are any cheerful? They should sing songs of praise. Are any among you sick? They should call for the elders of the church and have them pray over them, anointing them with oil in the name of the Lord. The prayer of faith will save the sick, and the Lord will raise them up; and anyone who has committed sins will be forgiven. Therefore confess your sins to one another, and pray for one another, so that you may be healed. The prayer of the righteous is powerful and effective. Elijah was a human being like us, and he prayed fervently that it might not rain, and for three years and six months it did not rain on the earth. Then he prayed again, and the heaven gave rain and the earth yielded its harvest (James 5:13-18).

Weekly Reading

The Israelites wander aimlessly in the desert, and God instructs them to use fringe as a prayer tool to remember the commandments—a form of prayer. The church in Thessalonica needs encouragement, and Paul suggests that they pray without ceasing. For the struggling Christians in his audience, James promotes prayer as a mainstay.

Though we often make prayer difficult, it doesn't have to be so. As James notes, as long as you offer up your life to God, it is prayer. It doesn't matter who you are or how you do it. The same is true with prayer beads; their use doesn't have to be hard. Many approaches exist.

In the first centuries after Jesus' death and resurrection, Christians faced many challenges. The fledgling church was just getting off the ground and finding its way in the world. We take for granted the stability of an established church with a codified Bible, creeds, and traditions. The early church had none of that. Given that the practice of Christianity was illegal until 313 CE, the world was a dangerous place for Christians. The threat of arrest and persecution surrounded the church. Followers of Christ lived in fear, and most churches met in secret.

This fear sets the context for James's letter. Though we don't know his specific audience, we do know from the first verse of the first chapter that James writes to Jewish Christians who are spread out across the land. From the rest of his letter we learn that these Christians struggled with the outside world, with religious leaders and teachers, and with one another. Their struggles have led to infighting, judgmentalism, temptation, and selfishness—much like the Israelites in the desert. We humans tend to buckle under stress and take it out on those around us, as well as on God. James addresses these behaviors with a mixture of tough love, gentle encouragement, and a healthy dose of optimism. Most of his letter offers advice and direction in various matters, but this week's scripture passage focuses on prayer.

James begins by answering several basic questions. *When* should people pray? When they are suffering, cheerful, or among the sick. In other words, at any time. Prayer connects us with God in the everyday matters of life, whether they are happy, sad, or in between. Through prayer we lift the mundane and extraordinary to God, who transforms them into moments of grace.

How can we pray? By singing songs of praise, anointing the sick with oil, confessing our sins, and praying for healing for one another. The ways of praying are vast. We can sit, stand, kneel, or dance. We can sing, shout aloud, or whisper. We can pray alone or with others. We can praise, confess, intercede, and give thanks. All of it is prayer—an offering to God.

Why should we pray? Because God hears our prayers and responds. Because our prayers will bring healing to situations in a variety of ways. We pray because our prayers are "powerful and effective." You can almost hear James shouting out that point.

Who should pray? All human beings. In case anyone questions this, James offers the example of Elijah, the Old Testament prophet, who prayed fervently. As the result of his prayers, explains James, there was no rain on the earth for three and a half years. God heard Elijah's prayers. James wants his readers to understand that Elijah was a human being like us. His prayers were effective not because he was somebody special. His prayers were effective because God hears prayer. Anyone and everyone should pray. Anyone and everyone will be heard by God.

James understands that the early Christians face enormous peril and hardship, and he empathizes with their situation. However, he also realizes that their fighting among themselves and casting judgment and being selfish only make their lives harder. As compassionately as he can, he exhorts them to rise above these challenges and live as Christ calls them to live: in peaceful community, loving God and one another. They will do this through prayer; through rich, fulfilling lives of prayer that encompass the joyous parts, the distressing parts, and all the mundane parts in between.

C. S. Lewis, Irish novelist and poet, made famous the saying that prayer doesn't change God; it changes us. James understood that and desires that these early Christians understand that as well. By offering their daily lives to God in prayer, they acknowledge that their lives are holy, worthy of God's love, time, and attention. And they will recognize the ways that God moves and acts in their lives, graciously working to redeem them and the world. Acknowledgment of God's gracious work in our lives frees *us* to create a life of prayer that is purely our own, one that represents who we are at any given point in time.

This week focuses on exploring a variety of ways to use beads in prayer. You can try any or all of them. You may even be inspired to develop your own. Think about what draws you to God or what you need at a given point in time, and let that determine how you pray with the beads. It is "all good."

One of the simplest uses of beads is to hold them. Just hold them. Lovely and simple. If you are a veteran pray-er, say whatever prayer you would normally say as you hold the beads. Let the feel of the beads keep you focused, grounded. If you are new to prayer, hold them while you experiment with ways of praying. Use the beads to remind you that God is with you and hearing you no matter what you say or do. Most importantly, for the grieved, the distressed, and the confused, hold the beads and feel God's comforting presence.

We can also use our beads to explore what we believe as Christians. There are many ways to do this.

Use Scripture

If you have a favorite passage of scripture or if you want to meditate on a particular verse or story in the Bible, you can do that with your beads. For a few short verses, try to memorize the verses and recite them as you follow the path of the beads. Or hold the beads as you read through the biblical story. You can also break the passage into four parts and use the beads to meditate on its deeper meaning. I have given an example of this option for this week's Prayer Bead Experience below. You can do something similar with the Creation story, the Psalms, the Beatitudes, or the parables. One book that I recommend to people who want to use scripture in connection with their beads is the book *Praying with Beads: Daily Prayers for the Christian Year* by Nan Lewis Doerr and Virginia Stem Owens. The authors have written a prayer bead devotion for every week of the Christian year. The devotions assign a distinct passage of scripture to each bead.

Use Our Faith

One of my favorite uses of the beads involves the exploration of the Christian faith. For example, many of us recite the Apostles' Creed during worship on a regular basis. But do we fully grasp its meaning? More specifically, do we understand the meaning the creed has for us personally? Take this creed—or any other—and break it down using the structure of the prayer beads. Use the first set of seven to focus on the statements about God the Father, the second set for Jesus Christ, the third for the Holy Spirit, and the fourth to consider how the creed impacts your life. Take time to concentrate on the individual phrases and apply them to your life.

In the past year, I wrote a prayer bead devotion on the Trinity (page 101), which I have included in "More Devotions for Prayer Beads." As Christians, we profess our faith in the triune God: God the Father, God the Son, and God the Holy Spirit—but the Trinity still remains one of the great mysteries of our faith. We would benefit from meditating on what it means to us. Prayer beads offer a tremendous opportunity to help us explore and deepen our understanding of what we, as Christians, believe. Experiment with ways to use your beads to meditate on a particular aspect of faith.

Use the Christian Calendar

Prayer beads work well in conjunction with the Christian calendar. I enjoy writing prayer bead devotions based on a specific season of the church year. Doing so helps me explore and better understand the mysteries of faith and the rhythm of our spiritual community. I have provided a sample devotion on Epiphany (page 99) in "More Devotions for Prayer Beads."

Use Life Circumstances

God accompanies us every moment of our lives. One way to experience God's presence encompasses lifting up individual life events. If we worry about something, we can use each of the week beads to talk to God about the cause of our anxiety. When we reach a cruciform bead, we may repeat words like these: "Fear not! For I am with you" (Isa. 41:10). The repetition of the phrase can serve as a powerful reminder of God's presence in the midst of our distress.

Similarly, if joy fills us, we can use the week beads to share our joy and offer thanks to God. At the cruciform beads, say, "Rejoice in the Lord always; again I will say, Rejoice" (Phil. 4:4).

We can use beads to offer our lives, our circumstances, and our faith to God. Our creativity in the use of the beads and in prayer in general expands our acceptance of life as a gift from our Creator God, a gift that will ultimately change us.

Prayer Bead Experience

This week's Prayer Bead Experience illustrates how to use prayer beads to offer your prayers to the Lord.

I provide two choices. I base the first devotion on the three times that Christ appears to his disciples following the Resurrection as recorded by John. It helps us understand what Jesus calls us to do as Christians. Using the beads invites us to slow down and consider how to apply Christ's call to our lives.

This devotion is longer than the previous experiences. However, do not get caught up in reading every word as printed. It is unnecessary to hold it like a script as you go through the devotion. I encourage reading it through once without beads to get a general idea of the devotion's purpose. Notice the key words (in bold type) that reflect the primary intent for each section of the devotion. When you begin to pray the devotion with beads in hand, you can pray freely using these key words as guides.

The second option invites you to write your own devotion and thereby develop your unique way of praying with beads. In addition, it provides a way for you to explore particular areas of faith or to pray about unique circumstances in your life. This time of writing can be a prayer in and of itself. I have provided a template below; however, feel free to create your own.

Following the Risen Christ

Cross: Gracious God,

Invitatory bead: We recall the time when Jesus stood among his disciples and said, "'Peace be with you!'" (John 20:19, NIV).

Resurrection bead: Grant us this peace as we reflect on Christ's call to us.

1st cruciform bead: Jesus, our risen Lord, we thank you for your gift of the Holy Spirit that enables us to **forgive** the sins of others, just as our sins have been forgiven (John 20:22-23).

Week beads, set 1: Use each bead to ask for forgiveness and to name those whom you need to forgive.

2nd cruciform bead: Jesus, our risen Lord, we know that you have called us to **believe** in you, even though we haven't seen you (John 20:29). We believe, Lord; help our unbelief.

Week beads, set 2: Use each bead to pray for strength of faith, particularly in those times when your faith has been weakened or threatened.

3rd cruciform bead: Jesus, our risen Lord, you have charged us with the responsibility to **feed** your sheep (John 21:17).

Week beads, set 3: Use each bead to meditate on the many ways you can be in ministry to Christ's sheep.

4th cruciform bead: Jesus, our risen Lord, you have called us simply to **follow** you (John 21:19).

Week beads, set 4: Use each bead to meditate on the ways in which you are called to follow Jesus.

Resurrection bead: By his resurrection, help us to remember Christ's call to us.

Invitatory bead: Pray the Lord's Prayer.

Cross: In the name of the Father, the Son, and the Holy Spirit. Amen.

Write Your Own Devotion

Cross:

Invitatory bead:

Resurrection bead:

1st cruciform bead:

Week beads, set 1:

2nd cruciform bead:

Week beads, set 2:

3rd cruciform bead:

Week beads, set 3:

4th cruciform bead:

Week beads, set 4:

Resurrection bead:

Invitatory bead:

Cross:

REFLECTION QUESTIONS

- Why do you pray? When do you pray?
- With what form of prayer do you feel most comfortable? least comfortable?
- In what areas have you experienced the truth of Lewis's statement (page 57) that prayer does not change God but instead changes the pray-er?
- How has using prayer beads made an impact on your prayer life so far?
- What other uses can you think of for prayer beads?
- What thoughts and reactions did you have to the Prayer Bead Experience?

WEEK FOUR

How to Listen with Prayer Beads

LISTEN

Prayer, we can now see, is communication,
in which God's word has the initiative and
we, at first, are simply listeners. Consequently,
what we have to do is, first, listen to God's word
and then, through that word, learn how to answer.

—HANS URS VON BALTHASAR

Prayer

SCRIPTURE PASSAGE

[The LORD] said, "Go out and stand on the mountain before the LORD, for the LORD is about to pass by." Now there was a great wind, so strong that it was splitting mountains and breaking rocks in pieces before the LORD, but the LORD was not in the wind; and after the wind an earthquake, but the LORD was not in the earthquake; and after the earthquake a fire, but the LORD was not in the fire; and after the fire a sound of sheer silence (1 Kings 19:11-12).

WEEKLY READING

Many of us rarely spend time listening in prayer, partly because we don't place enough emphasis on listening. We find it difficult to focus our minds when we are silent. In the quiet, we begin to create our grocery list or remind ourselves to return those overdue library books. I believe we feel uncomfortable with silence. We want to fill the quiet space with words and sound. And yet, as we read in First Kings, God is in the silence. There we can hear what God has to say to us.

By the ninth century BCE, when this story takes place, the kingdom of Israel has split into Israel and Judah. King

Ahab rules Israel. He has no desire to enforce the Mosaic laws under which the Israelites have lived and been governed for almost six hundred years. (I imagine the Israelites feverishly fingering their knotted fringe until it is threadbare in a valiant attempt to maintain the commandments under such circumstances.) Even worse, Ahab promotes the worship of Baal by building a temple dedicated to the pagan god, much to the delight of his wife, Jezebel. The queen, who is not native to Israel, supports 850 pagan prophets who expand pagan rituals and customs farther. Things do not look good for the Israelites.

As a prophet, Elijah is doing his best to improve the situation. He admonishes the king to change his ways, but Ahab is stubborn. Remember the reference to Elijah's prayers in Week Three? This is where that story plays out. As punishment for Ahab's resistance, Elijah declares a drought until he, Elijah, asks God to end it. And indeed, no rain falls—not even dew—in the entire land for three years. Still, Ahab refuses to budge.

God then sends Elijah to confront Ahab again. Elijah commands the king to hold a national assembly on Mount Carmel. Elijah makes it clear that the queen's pagan prophets should show up as well. When they arrive, Elijah challenges them to a prophetic duel of sorts. Both sides slaughter a bull and lay it out on wood. They then pray to their respective deities to see which one will set the wood on fire to make a proper sacrifice. Not surprisingly, Baal fails, but the Israelites' God comes through—an impressive showing. Elijah declares victory and has all the pagan prophets slain. And finally, it rains.

When Jezebel hears what has happened, she declares vengeance on Elijah, who flees in terror to the wilderness. By now, Elijah seems weary of being a prophet; in his exhaustion and terror he asks God to take away his life. But God recognizes the rantings of a tired man and ignores Elijah's request; instead, God sends an angel to pamper him. The angel's care is so effective that Elijah journeys for forty days and nights without additional food and water to a cave on Mount Horeb—the same place where Moses talked with God and received the commandments. There, the Lord meets Elijah and asks him what he is doing there.

Elijah responds in a torrent of complaint and self-pity: "I have been very zealous for the LORD, the God of hosts; for the Israelites have forsaken your covenant, thrown down your altars, and killed your prophets with the sword. I alone am left, and they are seeking my life, to take it away" (1 Kings 19:10). Elijah does not feel that God appreciates his predicament or recognizes how hard he has been working for the Lord. He wants God to know how much he resents his current situation.

But pay attention to God's response. God does not take on Elijah point by point or offer an explanation of "the big-picture" perspective—no words to comfort or calm Elijah. Instead, God instructs Elijah to come out of the cave and meet God who is about to "pass by."

Almost immediately, strange and scary things start to happen. First, a violent wind breaks apart pieces of the mountain. Then, an earthquake shakes the mountain. Lastly, a fire covers the mountain. All these events must have terrified poor Elijah But the writer of First Kings emphasizes that God is not in the wind; God is not in the earthquake; God is not in the fire.

This assertion makes me wonder if Elijah expected thunder and lightning or some other show of power as God passed by. After Elijah's passionate speech, I am curious to know if Elijah expected God to meet his passion with an equally fiery display. But God does not.

Instead, these calamities are followed by silence. That is it. Silence. The New Revised Standard Version refers to it as "sheer silence." In the New International Version, it is "a gentle whisper"; the King James Version describes it as a "still small voice." We get the picture: stillness, quiet, calm, peace. That is where God resides.

As I noted earlier, I used to struggle with prayer. I worried about what to say and the adequacy of my words—

not an uncommon problem. Many of us believe that prayer is strictly about what we have to say to God, as if by controlling our words we can control the outcome of the prayer, can control God's response.

Conversely, I think we can become overly talkative in prayer. I experience this aspect when I face a crisis. I quickly run to God and release a flurry of words. I can even spend a lot of time complaining about my sense of God's abandonment. I see a lot of Elijah in myself.

For all of Elijah's faithfulness, at times he got caught up in the drama and became self-involved. He failed to notice that God did not grant his suicidal wish but instead sent an angel to minister to him. By the time he speaks to God in verse 10, Elijah has become a bit narcissistic, even paranoid. Twice he cries that he is the *only* prophet left in Israel, failing to consider God's work in the lives of others. Indeed, God eventually points out that seven thousand faithful people remain in Israel. Elijah, hardly alone, does not know this fact because he is too busy talking.

Please hear me. We should bring our concerns to God. And we come to God when we need to rant, rave, complain, and cry out. We need to be able to do that. God wants us to be trusting enough to do that. God can handle whatever we bring, even our anger.

However, we often forget that prayer is a dialogue—a two-way conversation between us and God. Like any healthy, balanced conversation, we talk *and* listen. Only this approach allows us to remember that God is with us. Only then will we pause the rush of words and feelings before they overwhelm us. Only by talking *and* listening will we gain perspective and recognize that God is bigger than anything we have going on in our lives. Prayer beads can help us listen.

This book contains a lot of numbers. Jews use the fringe on the prayer shawl to remember the 613 commandments. The rosary was developed to remember the 150 Psalms or to pray the Lord's Prayer 150 times. One hundred knots on the prayer ropes of the Eastern church keep track of the repetitions of the Jesus Prayer. Protestant (or Anglican) prayer beads are made up of four sets of seven beads. Prayer beads are all about the numbers.

I did not recognize this bevy of numbers until I began leading workshops on prayer beads. I thought it was important to consider the use of prayer beads throughout history. History's perspective reflects the major role that prayer beads have played in connecting Christians to God for the past two thousand years. It also helps us understand how beads can enhance our own relationship with God.

As I reviewed each of these Judeo-Christian prayer tools, I realized that whether it's knotted fringe or beads or woolen knots, all these serve as tools for prayer and offer help in "counting" prayers. Whether we count commandments or repetitions of the Lord's Prayer or the Jesus Prayer, the beads help the pray-er track those repetitions.

As a Protestant, I was not raised to count prayers. We Protestants learn the Lord's Prayer and are encouraged to say our own prayers. We might even be lucky enough to receive coaching in the ways of prayer. But our Protestant upbringing does not teach us to count prayers.

Counting prayers actually facilitates listening. Think about it. We receive the words—commandments or a particular prayer. We do not have to spend time coming up with our own words. We run no risk of getting hung up on our own words or fumbling for what to say. And once we start praying the prayer at hand, our minds can relax. We can ride the rhythm of the repetition because we know that when we reach the forty-seventh commandment or the 134th repetition of the Lord's Prayer or even the ninth round of the Jesus Prayer, we stop concentrating on the words, which enables a different level of consciousness. At that point, we begin to listen.

I believe God desired this level of consciousness when commanding the Israelites to use the fringe to remember the commandments. Repeating the commandments over and over would help to quiet their minds and open them to listen to God's comforting words in the midst of the desert. The desert fathers and mothers came to this realization as they prayed the Psalms, fingering those pebbles on a daily basis. It became their way of praying unceasingly, their way of listening to God.

For me, listening to God in prayer is the true gift of prayer beads. We desperately desire to hear the voice of God in our noisy, busy lives. The prayer beads help us step out of the chaos. We can take a short prayer or a short verse of scripture, such as "Fear not, for I am with you" (Gen. 26:24, RSV) or "The Lord is my shepherd; I shall not want" (Ps. 23:1, KJV)—and repeat it with each bead. As we do, we shift our attention from the words and begin to listen for what God has to say to us. In the beginning, this style of prayer may seem awkward or uncomfortable. That is okay. If you stay with the practice, I can assure you that you will begin to feel calmer and realize a new way of connecting with God, an encounter with God's love. Like Elijah, you will find God in the "sheer silence."

Prayer Bead Experience

I designed this week's Prayer Bead Experience to help you practice using your beads to listen to God. As before, you have two options. You may use one or both devotions. "Be Still" incorporates silence as you follow the beads. "Draw Near" provides a short verse from scripture to repeat with each bead as a mantra (a short phrase or verse that you repeat). Use one of these each day. With either of them, once you develop a rhythm with your beads you might try a total of three revolutions of your beads to give your mind an opportunity to settle into this time with God. As you do, see if you can hear the "still small voice" of God.

Be Still

Cross: In the name of the Father, the Son, and the Holy Spirit. Amen.

Invitatory bead: (*take a deep, long breath*).

Resurrection bead: (*take another deep, long breath*).

Cruciform beads: "Be still, and know that I am God!" (Ps. 46:10).

Week beads: Use each bead to take a deep, long breath and *listen*.

(*If you have time, repeat this exercise for three revolutions of the prayer beads.*)

Resurrection bead: Christ is risen.
Invitatory bead: Thanks be to God.
Cross: Amen.

Draw Near

Cross: In the name of the Father, the Son, and the Holy Spirit. Amen.

Invitatory bead: "Go near and listen to all that the LORD our God says" (Deut. 5:27, NIV).

Resurrection bead: Christ lives so that I may draw near.

Cruciform beads: "Lord, I draw near."

Week beads: I am listening.

Resurrection bead: Christ lives so that I may draw near. Hallelujah.

Invitatory bead: Pray the Lord's Prayer.

Cross: In the name of the Father, the Son, and the Holy Spirit. Amen.

REFLECTION QUESTIONS

- How comfortable do you feel with silence?
- What do you think about Hans Urs von Balthasar's suggestion that prayer first entails listening and *then* answering?

- When have you spent time in prayer listening to God? What did you hear?
- How do prayer beads help you listen to God?
- What thoughts and reactions did you have to the Prayer Bead Experience?
- What have you learned about prayer beads as the result of this study? What surprised you? interested you?
- Do you plan to continue to use beads in your prayer time? Why or why not?

LEADER'S GUIDE

To deal with introductory information, I would suggest that you add a half hour either to the bead-making session (see page 89) or to the Week One meeting. One hour is sufficient for the weekly meetings thereafter. As the study leader, plan to arrive fifteen minutes early to prepare the room.

I recommend arranging chairs around a table so that group members are facing one another. This arrangement will facilitate dialogue as well as allow space for books, prayer beads, and notes. If a table is not available, arrange chairs in a circle.

I would also encourage you to think about ways to create a prayerful mood in the meeting room. Perhaps you can light a candle and play soft instrumental music in the background as members arrive or set up a small worship center with a cross and/or Bible. There is no need to make this complicated; simple settings often lend themselves to a spirit of prayer.

INTRODUCTORY OPENING

Since this will be the first time for these people to meet (unless they met previously to make prayer beads), take time to welcome each participant. Then, allow each person to introduce himself or herself. As part of the introductions, invite participants to

- Show their prayer beads to the group. Encourage them to talk about the beads: Did they make the set? If so, how did they choose the colors or design? What was meaningful about the process of making the set? If they did not make the prayer beads, where did they get them? Why did they choose that particular set? Was it given to them as a gift?

- Share what drew them to this study on prayer beads. How did they hear about the study? What about the study interested them? Have they prayed with beads before?

- Raise questions related to what they hope to receive from this study. Do they have particular questions about prayer beads? What are they wanting to learn?

Next, orient the group members to the study. Ask if anyone had specific questions about the Introduction. Then review the study outline: The study takes place over four weeks. The first two weeks' study are designed to answer the question "Why prayer beads?" Many people wonder why beads would be useful in prayer. And Protestants may wonder whether it is okay to pray with beads. The second two weeks are designed to answer the question "How do you use beads in prayer?" These weeks will provide a variety of ways to use prayer beads.

Each week includes a Scripture Passage, Weekly Reading, Prayer Bead Experience, and Reflection Questions. The Prayer Bead Experiences offer the participants a chance to use their prayer beads in many ways.

Encourage the participants to do the following:

- take 30–45 minutes each week to read the assigned Scripture Passage and Weekly Reading;
- write down any questions they may have and bring them to the study meetings;
- spend at least five minutes each day practicing the Prayer Bead Experience; and
- review responses to the Reflection Questions.

This will ensure that each person benefits as much as possible from the study.

Assure the participants that there are no right or wrong ways to use prayer beads. This study introduces people to a variety of ways to use beads in prayer and gives participants an opportunity to experiment using the Prayer Bead Experiences. Some of the experiences may be more comfortable or compelling than others, and that is okay. The experiences may inspire participants to come up with their own ways of using beads in prayer. Ultimately, the beads are intended to help people draw closer to God. Hopefully, the beads will help them gain a certain comfort level with prayer, experience God in a new way, feel more connected to God, and learn to "listen" to God.

In closing, ask the group members to hold their prayer beads in their hands. Explain that you will bless the beads using the following prayer:

Creator God,
You love us enough to call us into your presence through prayer, and for that we give thanks.

We thank you for the many ways in which we can connect with you, including through the use of prayer beads.

We ask your blessing upon these beads. May they remind us of your loving presence, draw us into prayer, focus our time with you, and help us to listen to what you have to say to us.

We pray this in Jesus' name. Amen.

WEEKLY FORMAT

Opening

When all participants arrive and find a seat, take a moment to help everyone transition from the noise and rush of daily life to this time of reflection and discussion. Encourage participants to hold their prayer beads, close their eyes, and take three deep breaths. This does not have to be formal; let it be an opportunity to relax and be still in God's presence.

Pray the week's Prayer Bead Experience together

Each week identify one person to be the leader. The leader will read the Prayer Bead Experience out loud while participants hold their prayer beads and follow along with each bead. When the leader comes to the cruciform bead, he or she will read the prayer for that bead aloud, then allow time for silence as the participants pray silently while fingering each of the seven week beads. After providing a sufficient amount of time for the participants to pray with all seven week beads (about one minute), the leader will read the prayer for the next cruciform bead out loud. Continue in this way through the conclusion of the prayer. For those weeks that offer two experiences, choose one. Another option comes in inviting a person who has written his or her own prayer bead devotion to lead the group in praying it.

Set the context for the lesson

Look ahead to the upcoming week to familiarize yourself with the content. Then use the following suggested script to help prepare the group for each week's lesson.

Week One: Many people wonder how prayer beads would be useful in prayer. Others wonder if it is okay to use objects to pray. To get us started, we will look at the story of the Israelites in the desert and read how God provided them with a prayer tool. Our reflection on this passage will open our discussion on prayer beads.

Week Two: When talking about prayer beads, people often ask whether Protestants can use prayer beads. This week, we will consider Paul's direction to "pray without ceasing" and our difficulty in observing this practice. We will look at various tools the early Christians used to help them pray without ceasing.

Week Three: There are many reasons and ways to pray, as Paul describes in First Thessalonians. Similarly, there are many reasons and ways to use beads in prayer. This week, we will consider different ideas for incorporating beads into prayer.

Week Four: One of the greatest ways to deepen our relationship with God is by taking time to listen to what God has to say to us. At a time when he felt particularly lonely, the prophet Elijah learned that he only had to listen to know that God was with him. Prayer beads can help us listen. This week we will explore ways of using prayer beads to listen to God.

Leader's Guide

Read the week's Scripture Passage aloud

After a volunteer reads the scripture aloud, invite the group members to take a moment for prayerful consideration of the scripture, or you can say, "The word of God for the people of God." They would respond by saying, "Thanks be to God." Then invite participants to state aloud any thoughts or insights they received while listening.

Review the Reflection Questions

You may choose to take each question in order. Read it aloud and allow time for the group members' responses. Another option would entail your inviting group members to speak about the questions they found most thought-provoking.

You may not have the answers to all the questions. That is okay. Do the best you can and feel free to invite responses from others in the group. If you have the opportunity, consider reviewing other resources on prayer beads using the list provided in the Resources section (page 105). If you do not know the answer to a question, invite group members to do additional research on their own.

The challenge in working with groups comes in finding a balance between the extroverts and the introverts. Inevitably, you will have members who are talkative and feel comfortable speaking up while others are shy and quiet. It is important to create an environment in which every participant feels encouraged and comfortable to share if he or she chooses without putting undue pressure on those who prefer to remain silent. If you find yourself leading a group that is unusually quiet, experiment with ways of encouraging each member to participate. Perhaps you could ask the members to take turns reading and/or responding to the question aloud.

Share observations from the Prayer Bead Experience

Review one or all of the questions below or encourage participants to share thoughts about the experience.

- How did the experience help in your understanding of the use of prayer beads?
- How did the experience help in your understanding of different ways of praying?
- How did the experience aid your understanding of connecting and communicating with God?

Closing

Choose one of the following options:
- Invite a participant to lead the group through a prayer that he/she has developed to use with beads (it may

work best to arrange this ahead of time to give the person some advance notice).

- Invite the group members to use their beads to pray the following prayer:

Cross: In the name of the Father, the Son, and the Holy Spirit. Amen.

Invitatory bead: Gracious God,

Resurrection bead: who loved us enough to reveal yourself through your Son,

1st cruciform bead: We thank you for what we have learned from this week's Scripture Passage and Weekly Reading.

Week beads, set 1: *In silence*, use each bead to lift up any insights you have received from the week's Scripture Passage and Weekly Reading.

2nd cruciform bead: We thank you for revealing new ways of praying through the Prayer Bead Experience.

Week beads, set 2: *In silence*, use each bead to give thanks for any new ways of praying you have received from the Prayer Bead Experience.

3rd cruciform bead: We ask that you guide us in the week to come as we continue to seek ways of being with you.

Week beads, set 3: *In silence*, use each bead to ask for guidance and insight as you go through the next week and/or prepare for next week's lesson.

4th cruciform bead: Finally, Lord, we ask that you be with each of us as we go through the next week and bring us together again at our next meeting.

Week beads, set 4: *In silence*, use each bead to pray for each member of your group.

Resurrection bead: In the name of your Son, Jesus Christ, who died so that we might live,

Invitatory bead: we pray.

Cross: Amen.

MAKING PRAYER BEADS

If you plan to make prayer beads with your group, I recommend you set aside about one hour. If you plan to discuss the Introduction as well, set aside one and one-half to two hours. This session would be prior to the Week One session.

To maximize your time, review the following instructions. Consider watching the instructional video found at http://abeadnaprayer.wordpress.com/2013/05/02/video-how-to-make-prayer-beads/, prior to the bead-making session. Even better, by making a set of prayer beads in advance you will ensure that you are prepared to lead your group members through this activity and have a sample set to show them. You will serve as their inspiration!

Approaches and Skill Levels

- If you have plenty of time for the bead-making session, I recommend purchasing beads in a variety of colors and allowing the participants to create their own designs. This approach can encourage people to give thought to the color and composition of this prayer tool.

- If your time is limited, however, I suggest you prepare "kits" in advance. Each kit would contain all the materials one person would need to complete a set of prayer beads, except for the tools and crimp tubes. You might offer some variety among the kits—such as two or three different color combinations—to allow for some choice and individualization.

You will also want to consider the participants' *skill level* when it comes to working with beads.

- If you have one or two *experienced participants* who have worked with beads and the rest have *little or no background*, I recommend that you attach the crosses to the wire ahead of time (see Step 1, page 94). This saves time and frustration and makes the prayer bead-making session much more enjoyable.

- If you are working with a group of *skilled beaders,* they may feel quite capable of attaching the cross to the wire themselves.

In addition to the beads, I recommend having a small bowl or tray for each participant to collect his or her beads or to hold the kit as the prayer beads are assembled.

The Crimp Tubes

Successful completion of prayer beads is due, in large part, to the crimp tubes. Although tiny, these tubes serve a critical function in the formation of the prayer beads. Allow me to stress three aspects:

1. Distribute the crimp tubes separately from the other prayer bead materials. The reason for this is simple: The tiny crimp tubes can easily get lost if mixed with a larger bag or bowl of beads. Whether I use pre-assembled kits or allow participants to choose their own beads, I always pass out the crimp tubes myself, carefully placing them in front of the participants and drawing their attention to them. It might help to assign a crimp-tube distributor.

2. Make sure participants understand the placement of the crimp tubes on their wires. They must add the crimp tubes to the wire early on in the process rather than adding them later. If someone strings all the beads on the wire and realizes he or she has forgotten to add the crimp tube, that person will have to undo the set and start all over.

3. Be prepared to provide assistance to participants who need help threading the crimp tubes onto the wire. Again, you might consider having someone who distributes and provides assistance with the crimp tubes.

The Tools

A crucial piece to making prayer beads is the tools. The good news is that beading requires only two tools: chain nose pliers and side wire cutters. The even better news is that you can find both of these tools at a craft store, a hardware store, or in your family's toolbox. If you have no beading experience, I would encourage you to practice using the tools before leading the group through this activity.

I recommend that you identify one person to be in charge of "tying off" the prayer beads (if you have more than one person who can do this, all the better). This person sits at a table with the tools. As participants finish stringing their beads together, they can bring their sets to the tool person. The tool person can then complete Steps 13–14.

Room Setup

Making prayer beads can be a good group-building activity. People seem to enjoy talking and bonding with one another as they string their beads. I recommend using round or rectangular tables where people can sit facing one another. If that is not possible, a classroom or training room setup will work as well.

At the front, side, or back of the room, set up a table where you can lay out all of the bead-making supplies or kits. This may be the same table where the identified tool person sits to tie off the prayer beads.

Consider adding other enhancements to this experience such as:

- a music player available to play Taizé or other soft background music;
- completed sets of prayer beads around the room for people to see;
- snacks or beverages.

Making a set of prayer beads is fairly easy, even if you have no prior beading experience. I have provided instructions below. These instructions are illustrated in a video at http://abeadnaprayer.wordpress.com/2013/05/02/video-how-to-make-prayer-beads/.

The materials listed below can be purchased at a local craft store. My company, Prayerworks Studio, also offers kits, which include the necessary materials (but not the tools). You may purchase the kits at www.prayerworksstudio.etsy.com. Use the discount code BOOK20 to receive 20% off your purchase.

Materials Needed

5 large (10mm–12mm) beads
29 medium (8mm–10mm) beads
36 seed (size #6 or #8) beads
1 cross or other pendant
2 crimp tubes (size 2 x 2)
20–24 inches of wire (49 strand, .18 or .19 inches)

Tools Required

1 pair of chain nose pliers
1 set of side wire cutters

Instructions

L = Large bead (cruciform and invitatory)

M = Medium bead (week and resurrection)

s = seed bead

Step 1: Thread one of the crimp tubes onto the wire, then add the cross. (See figure 1.) Thread the end of the wire back up through the crimp tube. This will leave you with the two ends of the wire coming out of the crimp tube: the primary length of wire and a smaller "tail," about one inch in length. Using the pliers, squeeze the crimp tube until it is flattened. (See figure 2.)

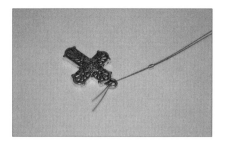

FIGURE I

FIGURE 2

STEP 2: String the beads in the following pattern, taking them all the way down so that the first bead aligns with the crimp tube that sits above the cross. (Note: make sure the beads cover both of the wires—the primary wire and the extra piece that extends from the top of the cross):

s L s M s L s

STEP 3: String the crimp tube (*this is a critical step!*).

STEP 4: String the first section of week beads in the following pattern: s M (7 times), then 1 s. It will look like this:

s M s M s M s M s M s M s M s

STEP 5: String 1 L bead.

STEP 6: String the second section of week beads by repeating Step 4.

STEP 7: String 1 L bead.

STEP 8: String the third section of week beads by repeating Step 4.

STEP 9: String 1 L bead.

STEP 10: String the fourth section of week beads by repeating Step 4.

STEP 11: Take the end of the wire and thread it back through the crimp tube that was added in STEP 3 (the wire will be heading back toward the cross; see figure 3). Thread it through the crimp tube, the seed bead, the large bead, the seed bead, and the medium bead so that it comes out from the bottom of the medium bead.

FIGURE 3

STEP 12: Pull the wire tightly, adjusting the beads as necessary to remove any slack in the wire and to ensure that the wire is completely covered up by the beads (figure 4). This is a good time to count all the beads and double check your pattern to be sure the beads are in the order you desire. If not, make the necessary changes before proceeding to the next step.

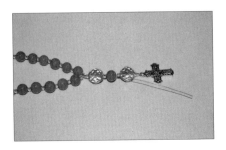

Figure 4

Step 13: Using a pair of chain nose pliers, flatten the crimp tube as tightly as possible.

Step 14: Using a set of side wire cutters, cut the remaining wire off as close to the beads as possible.

Completed Set
Enjoy your beads! Blessings!

MORE DEVOTIONS FOR PRAYER BEADS

I INCLUDE THE following devotions to show other ways to use beads in prayer. Do not get caught up in reading every word exactly as printed unless you want to. Read the devotion through once without your beads to get a general idea of the devotion's purpose. Then pray freely.

A DEVOTION FOR EPIPHANY

This devotion celebrates the season that follows Christmas and recalls the wise men's journey to worship the Christ child.

   Cross: In the name of the Father, the Son, and the Holy Spirit. Amen.
   Invitatory bead: "When they saw the star, they were overjoyed. On coming to the house, they saw the child with his mother Mary, and they bowed down and worshiped him. Then they opened their treasures and presented him with gifts of gold, frankincense and myrrh" (Matt. 2:10-11, NIV).
   Resurrection bead: Christ is born!

1st cruciform bead: Lord, you called the magi to you, sending them a star to guide them to Bethlehem. Help us to recognize the ways in which you call us into a relationship with you.

Week beads, set 1: Use each bead to listen for, recognize, and consider the many ways in which God calls you to a relationship.

2nd cruciform bead: Lord, the magi obediently and gladly followed your star to Bethlehem, fulfilling your plan for them.

Week beads, set 2: Use each bead to consider the ways in which you can joyfully and obediently follow God's will for you.

3rd cruciform bead: Lord, upon seeing your son, Jesus, the magi fell on their knees and worshiped him.

Week beads, set 3: Use each bead to offer your praise and worship to God.

4th cruciform bead: Lord, having worshiped you, the magi freely and joyfully offered their gifts to your Son, in response to your gift of love to the world.

Week beads, set 4: Use each bead to consider the gifts you can offer to God, in thanks for God's gift of love for you.

Resurrection bead: Christ is born! Alleluia!

Invitatory bead: Pray the Lord's Prayer.

Cross: In the name of the Father, the Son, and the Holy Spirit. Amen.

A DEVOTION ON THE TRINITY

As Christians we believe that God is one in three persons: God the Father, God the Son, and God the Holy Spirit. But what does that concept mean? In particular, what impact does it have on our faith? This devotion helps us consider this mystery of the triune God, especially as it informs our relationship with others.

Cross: Loving God,

Invitatory bead: be with me in this time of prayer.

Resurrection bead: Open my heart and mind to the presence of your son, Jesus Christ. Guide my thoughts and words, and fill me with your Spirit.

1st cruciform bead: I pray to God the Father . . .

Week beads, set 1: Use each bead to praise God the Father (*praise and thanks*).

2nd cruciform bead: I pray to Jesus Christ, God's only Son, our Lord . . .

Week beads, set 2: Use each bead to ask Jesus Christ for forgiveness and help (*confession and prayer concerns*).

3rd cruciform bead: I pray to the Holy Spirit . . .

Week beads, set 3: Use each bead to ask the Holy Spirit to work in and through you (*such as, praying to be a better disciple, to spend more time in prayer, to discern God's will for you, etc.*).

4th cruciform bead: I pray that I may better understand who God is and how the Trinity can serve as a model for my relationship with others . . .

Week beads, set 4: Use each bead to meditate on how the Trinity—God the Father, God the Son, and God the Holy Spirit—can serve as a model for human relationships and for the church, celebrating the diversity of each member while coming together in perfect union.

Resurrection bead: Christ is risen and invites me into this perfect union.

Invitatory bead: Pray the Lord's Prayer.

Cross: In the name of the Father, the Son, and the Holy Spirit. Amen.

A Devotion for Use by Children

This is one example of a basic prayer for use by children. I offer two formats: one for a chaplet (17 or 18 beads) and one for a full set of prayer beads (33 or 34 beads).

For a chaplet

Invitatory bead: Dear God,

Resurrection bead: thank you for loving me.

1st cruciform bead: Thank you for . . .

Week beads, set 1: Instruct your child to use each bead to name something for which he or she is thankful.

2nd cruciform bead: Please bless . . .

Week beads, set 2: Instruct the child to use each bead to name someone.

Resurrection bead: Thank you, God, for loving me.

Invitatory bead: Amen.

For a full set of prayer beads

Invitatory bead: Dear God,

Resurrection bead: thank you for loving me.

1st cruciform bead: Thank you for . . .

Week beads, set 1: Instruct the child to use each bead to name something for which he or she is thankful.

2nd cruciform bead: Please bless . . .

Week beads, set 2: Instruct the child to use each bead to name a family member.

3rd cruciform bead: Please bless . . .

Week beads, set 3: Have the child use each bead to name a friend, church member, or someone else.

4th cruciform bead: I wanted to tell you about . . .

Week beads, set 4: Allow your child to use each bead to tell God whatever is on his or her heart.

Resurrection bead: Thank you, God, for loving me.

Invitatory bead: Amen.

For more devotions, I invite you to visit my blog:
www.abeadnaprayer.wordpress.com

RESOURCES

THE FOLLOWING WEBSITES will satisfy your interest in purchasing prayer beads or the materials to make your own prayer beads and in learning more about this prayer tool.

PRAYER BEADS

www.prayerworksstudio.etsy.com (use discount code BOOK20 to receive 20% off your purchase)
www.etsy.com/shop/prayerbedes
www.fullcirclebeads.com
www.solitariesofdekoven.org/store.html

BEADS AND MATERIALS

www.firemountaingems.com
www.goodybeads.com
www.shipwreckbeads.com

MORE INFORMATION

www.abeadnaprayer.wordpress.com
www.kingofpeace.org/prayerbeads.htm
www.kimberlywinston.wordpress.com
www.prayerbedes.com

To read more about Protestant or other types of prayer beads, consider the following:

Books

Bauman, Lynn C. *The Anglican Rosary.* Telephone, TX: Praxis, 2003.

Brown, Patricia D. *Paths to Prayer: Finding Your Own Way to the Presence of God.* San Francisco: Jossey-Bass. 2003.

Doerr, Nan Lewis, and Virginia Stem Owens. *Praying with Beads: Daily Prayers for the Christian Year.* Grand Rapids, MI: William B. Eerdmans Publishing Company, 2007.

Ellsworth, Wendy. *Beading—the Creative Spirit: Finding Your Sacred Center through the Art of Beadwork.* Woodstock, VT: SkyLight Paths Publishing, 2009.

Kasten, Patricia Ann. *Linking Your Beads: The Rosary's History, Mysteries, and Prayers.* Huntington, IN: Our Sunday Visitor Publishing Division, 2011.

Ward, J. Neville. *Five for Sorrow, Ten for Joy: A Consideration of the Rosary.* Cambridge, MA: Cowley Publications, 1985.

Wiley, Eleanor, and Maggie Oman Shannon. *A String and a Prayer: How to Make and Use Prayer Beads.* Newburyport, MA: Red Wheel/Weiser, 2002.

Winston, Kimberly. *Bead One, Pray Too: A Guide to Making and Using Prayer Beads.* Harrisburg, PA: Morehouse Publishing, 2008.

NOTES

1. I recognize that "The Full Circle" prayer is very similar to the ACTS formula for prayer: Adoration, Confession, Thanksgiving, and Supplication. My modification is based on my belief that our encounter with God necessarily—and almost involuntarily—begins with praise and ends with thanksgiving. These are the natural offerings to a God who is perfectly good. In the midst, we would confess our unworthiness and seek God's assistance. We see this played out in Isaiah 6. Isaiah describes a vision in which he encounters the Lord. In that encounter he praises God ("Holy, holy, holy is the Lord of hosts); confesses to God ("Woe is me!"); intercedes for his people ("I live among a people of unclean lips"); and ends with thanks ("Yet my eyes have seen the King, the Lord of hosts!"). End on a high note! However, as I have said before, there is no right or wrong way to pray. If you are familiar with the ACTS prayer and like it, I encourage you to use it with your prayer beads instead.

2. Many people perceive the concept of praying unceasingly as an unattainable goal and one that may cause unnecessary angst for those of us who cannot do it.

I do not think that was Paul's intent. In Matthew 22:36-40, Jesus tells us that the greatest commandment is to love God with "all" of our heart, soul, and mind, and to love our neighbors as ourselves. This implies that we devote our entire being to loving. However, God recognizes that this does not come naturally, nor is it easy for us to do. It is a process, one that may take a lifetime. Prayer is a significant part of that process.

3. John F. Thornton and Susan B. Varenne, eds. *Faith and Freedom: An Invitation to the Writings of Martin Luther* (New York: Vintage Books, 2002), 328.

4. Doerr, Nan Lewis and Virginia Stem Owens. *Praying with Beads: Daily Prayers for the Christian Year.* Wm. B. Eerdmans Publishing Co, Grand Rapids, MI: 2007, viii.

5. Ibid, ix.

ABOUT THE AUTHOR

KRISTEN E. VINCENT is the owner and principal artisan of Prayerworks Studio, which specializes in making handcrafted prayer beads and other prayer tools. She speaks widely on prayer and prayer beads and enjoys leading retreats. She is also a freelance writer and maintains a blog (www.abeadnaprayer.wordpress.com). Kristen has a Master of Theological Studies from Duke Divinity School and is participating in the Academy for Spiritual Formation (Academy #34). She is a native Texan who lives in Georgia with her husband, Max, a United Methodist minister, and their son, Matthew. She loves dark chocolate, the Texas Hill Country, stories about the early church, and working from home in her pajamas.